FOREWORD

At a time when the Town and Community of Fraserburgh is celebrating the fourth century of its inauguration, it is natural that Brochers should cast their thoughts back on the road they have come and remember the cloud of witnesses who served their day and generation faithfully and well and whose lives bear testimony to the faith that was in them and the spirit in which they were bred and brought up.

One has only to glance through the names in this book to realise the distinguished mark so many of our fellow citizens have made in so many walks of life and in such dedicated service to mankind these four hundred years, not only at home but in the far corners of the earth. From our small community we have sent out missionaries, explorers, diplomats, men of business, doctors, scholars, even a poet or two, to make the world a happier, richer and truer place. That work is still far from complete; in facing up to it we of today may take courage and inspiration for the future from the achievements of Brochers in days gone by.

There is a story told of an old Broch worthy whose nightly prayer was that 'the Lord wad gie us a guid conceit o' oursels', inviting the retort that no prayer has ever been so abundantly answered.

The following pages give chapter and verse to prove that our pride in our forebears is amply justified.

David Murison

Famous Brochers

Printed in Fraserburgh

by

A. J. & D. R. Cooper

ERRATUM
———
Page 16
For Forbes read Fraser

Ab39F1
486187

ISBN   0 9516964 1 6   FAMOUS BROCHERS

INDEX

GEORGE ANDERSON

When John Anderson, a housebuilder in Fraserburgh, married Jean Lunan, little did they suspect that their son would reach the giddy heights he did.

George Anderson was born on 26th March, 1845 and attended both the Parish School and the Free Church School leaving aged 12 with "good penmanship and an uncommon ability with figures" to enter an apprenticeship with the North of Scotland Bank in Saltoun Square. In three short years he so impressed his employers that he was promoted, aged 15, to the position of accountant to the branch. This was only the start of his meteoric rise to fame and his promotions came rapidly. At 18 he was moved to Banff to take up the position of accountant; at 21 he held the same position in the Elgin branch; at 23 he was transferred to Peterhead again as accountant, all the while to bigger branches, gaining experience all the way. He remained in Peterhead until 1873 when, aged 28, he took up the post of Agent with the bank at Huntly, being transferred in 1879 to the same position in the Dundee branch, the largest branch outside Aberdeen. It was inevitable that in 1888 he was recalled by head office in Aberdeen to take up the post of assistant manager, until in July, 1889 and at 44 years of age, he was promoted to manager.

It is worth noting that due to poor management by his predecessors, the bank had to write off its entire reserve fund of £213,000 in 1887. This dramatic move was brought about by overlending to the fishing industries, predominantly to the fishcurers in and around Aberdeen. By 1898 George Anderson had taken the reserve fund back up to a healthy balance of £125,000 and had increased the share value from £5.00 to £10.00. Such was the confidence bestowed in George by his friends in the Broch that a great many of them invested substantial sums of money in his bank when prices were depressed, and made a fortune later on after he turned their finances round. There is no record of this being "insider trading" but perhaps he was "looking after his ain folk" none the less.

In November, 1898, he was invited to take up the position of Treasurer to the Bank of Scotland, the premier banking post in the country. This was an unusual promotion, for George was not an employee of that body and was employed by a provincial bank. What made the appointment secure however was his impeccable record in the industry and the miracles he had worked along the way. In a 15 year period in Edinburgh he increased the assets of the bank by 50%, raised dividends by 66% to 20%, and increased the reserve fund by 100%. Over the duration of his appointment he issued 25 annual reports, each of which bettered, in every respect, its predecessor. Anyone who is involved in business of any nature will testify to the extreme rarity, and accomplishment, of this feat.

Not satisfied that his contribution to banking was a reasonable mark to make in the world, he was also noted as a linguist, music lover, raconteur, wit and good companion. He had opportunities to exercise his linguistic skills on many occasions, having travelled to every European country both in the course of business and pleasure as well as to America and Canada and the entire coast of North Africa — a long way from his native Broch.

He married his cousin Mary in 1870 and they built a house at Beechmount in Murrayfield, Edinburgh, in 1900 as their family home. This was no *pied-a-terre* for it is recorded as having cost £30,000 and was surely the last word in elegance and taste.

He was also an active member of the Free Church and was ordained a deacon in Elgin while serving in that town. Despite on many occasions being asked to take higher office, he declined, preferring to stay closer to his friends. In addition to this George was also a Governor of Donaldson's Hospital, a Director of Scottish Widow's Life Assurance Society, a Justice of the Peace in both the county of Aberdeen and Midlothian and from 1874 to 1879 held Queen Victoria's Commission as Captain of the Aberdeenshire (Huntly) Volunteers.

This was not George's only "acquaintance" with royalty for in 1905 he was knighted by King Edward, the first Brocher to receive this honour, adopting for himself the motto "Stand Sure". He was honoured both in Edinburgh and Fraserburgh and was greatly pleased by the banquet and speeches in his honour, given in the local town hall on the 7th of August of that year.

He was further honoured in 1902 and also in 1911, by being asked to act as Deputy Usher of the White Rod of Scotland at the coronations of both Edward VII and George V in London and Westminster respectively. He is recorded by Cranna as "the greatest man that Fraserburgh has produced", and if financial reward is a yardstick, then suffice to say that his salary was greater than that of the Prime Minister.

He is remembered in Fraserburgh, not only for the achievements noted in this brief biography, but also for his bequests to the town. The most notable of these are the clocks in the steeple of the South Kirk, the stained glass windows in honour of his parents in the High Kirk, and the Gold Medal he donated to the school in

1909 for presentation to the dux. The first recipient of this medal is recorded as being one Harry Ronald, who presumably inspired by this award went on to greater things.

No greater tribute can be given to this man than the Cranna eulogy, and the writer predicts with some certainty that the example set by Sir George will serve as inspiration for aspiring scions of business for years to come.

DR. JEAN BENZIE (1899-1987)

Dr. Jean Benzie was a medical missionary who devoted more than thirty years of her life to the womenfolk of India.

Born in 1899 the elder daughter of Mr. William Benzie, founder of the drapery firm of Benzie & Miller, Jean Benzie graduated in 1924 in medicine and surgery from Aberdeen University, moving immediately to London to carry out additional training in midwifery.

In 1925 she was accepted by the Baptist Missionary Society and spent her first year as a medical missionary at Farrer Hospital, Bhiwani, in the Punjab. The next two years she worked at Palwal, followed by a further two years at Dholpur. In 1933 she returned to Farrer Hospital where she remained until her retiral in 1956.

The Farrer Hospital contained 100 beds but often admitted more patients, the extra beds being put out on the verandahs. There was also a training school in the hospital in which Dr. Benzie worked with Dr. Farrer and a Dr. Bisset. On the retiral of her mentors, Doctor Jean took over the running of the entire establishment.

A tireless and devoted worker, she soon built up the reputation of being a highly skilled surgeon. Patients travelled great distances to have operations carried out by Dr. Benzie or to have their babies delivered by her.

In India in the first half of this century women were very much second class citizens, totally subjugated to their husbands and repressed by their customs. As a doctor and midwife, Dr. Benzie visited the homes of both rich and poor, gaining a marvellous insight into everyday family life. Her lecture, published in the "Fraserburgh Herald" in 1931 makes interesting reading, giving a concise and detailed account of the Indian woman's life at that time.

On furlough from her work in India, Dr. Benzie was in great demand as a speaker at the local churches and Women's Guilds, giving many interesting lectures on her work as a medical missionary.

Jean Benzie was an extremely active and respected member of the local Bhiwani church and being well known in the area she was often invited to attend civic functions. An excellent linguist and a gifted pianist, her musical evenings were a highlight of the local social calendar and were long remembered by her many friends and admirers.

Elected to the governing body of the Ludhiana Hospital, another post she filled with honour, she was awarded the Kaiser-i-Hind medal for her service to India prior to her retiral from the service.

On her return to Fraserburgh she continued her work for the Church, acting as temporary organist at several churches and taking on the role of mission secretary for the Baptist Churches in the North of Scotland. She also served as a locum doctor in the area and continued to give many talks on her life's work in India.

Dr. Benzie died at Fraserburgh Hospital on 21st February, 1987, after a long and distinguished medical career. She had a full life of Christian service that surely earns the commendation: "Well done, good and faithful servant".

JOHN CLARK

In Dr. John Clark, Fraserburgh gave the world one of the greatest mathematical minds of his, or indeed any other age. Born on 9th April, 1864 he attended the local Academy, which was then located in Mid Street. A mere stripling of 15 years, he won a scholarship for Aberdeen University graduating aged 19 with First Class Honours. He won the Ferguson Scholarship for Mathematics which at that time was the premier academic accolade in Scotland. He went on to win the Fullarton prize at Aberdeen University, which brought together in competition the best mathematicians in the north, by a considerable margin. After achieving top honours at Cambridge, he became the first doctor of science at Aberdeen University where he lectured with uncommon distinction.

From Aberdeen he then moved to Egypt, taking up the mathematics chair at Cairo Polytechnic College where he lived and worked until his death on 10th January, 1911.

John was also a linguist extraordinaire, getting his tongue masterfully round French, German, Italian and Arabic. He was honoured by the Societe Scientifique de France after his publication in France of a defiinitive work in nomography, a new science inter-relating astronomy and engineeering with detailed and minute calculations.

Like many greatly gifted men, his talents were not only professionally based. He had a reputation as an accomplished public speaker and was a noted humourist as well as being considerably talented as a violinist.

On the sporting front his ability shone through on the football field and also as an oarsman, but perhaps he shone brightest as a swimmer, being the founder of the first official swimming club in town.

His name lives on in the Academy having made a bequest to the school of the Clark medal, which was to be awarded to the mathematical dux each year.

JOHN CRANNA

Best remembered as being the author of "Fraserburgh — Past and Present" which prodigious work, published in 1914, is still the best known and most used work of reference on our town in all its facets, even today. The covers of this crusty tome shelter a virtually complete history of Fraserburgh in all its considerable glory. Not considered bed-time reading by any except registered insomniacs, it is however a worthwhile contribution to Scottish history, as well as a damned good read!

Cranna was born in 1853 to John Cranna, the leading haulier of his day in town and latterly the Ballast Master of the harbour steelyard. He was indentured to Robert Anderson the Solicitor, one of the Philorth Andersons, and upon completion of his apprenticeship he went to work for Alex Bruce, the noted fishcurers, as a cashier. He learned the basis of the herring trade both at Bruce's and under the tutelage of Helm Schroder in Stettin, Germany. This knowledge was to serve him, and the Broch well, in the future.

On his return from Germany he quickly fell back into Broch life, or perhaps the Broch had to accelerate to meet him.

He became in short order a prominent member of the Debating & Kindred Societies, President of the Musical Society and an enthusiastic member of both the cricket and golf clubs, the latter of which he captained many times. Obviously a man of high energy he was also a serving member of the Fraserburgh Company of Artillery Volunteers, rising to the rank of Honorary Captain. Choirmaster of the church that conducted his own funeral, the Parish Kirk, upon his death at 28 Victoria Street, on the 24th of March, 1932, he left a widow, one son and four daughters.

As man cannot live on voluntary work, he exerted his business energies in the service of the town. Thanks to a report prepared by John in 1876 on the herring trade, Sir Alexander Anderson commissioned him to compile a variety of statistical reports which enabled the redoubtable Sir Alexander to obtain loans to develop the harbour.

In October, 1878, John Cranna was appointed Harbour Treasurer, (and who knew more about the business), keeping the position for fifty years. As a demonstration of his effectiveness, in 1879 harbour revenue was £7,700 while it rose under his careful husbandry to an incredible £800,000.

While most men would be happy and proud to accomplish any of the above in one lifetime, such is the mark of the man that he was also well known and respected nationally as a journalist, contributing worthy articles to papers on both sides of the Border.

ALEXANDER FORBES 7th Laird of Philorth

Back in the dim and distant days of the sixteenth century, in 1530 to be precise, this hardy chiel consigned himself to the immortal history of the Broch by becoming our first convicted murderer. Alexander, then Laird of Philorth and Brux and grandfather of the founder of the town, killed one David Scott, an Aberdonian, in a fight that ensued from some argument between his father-in-law the Provost of Aberdeen, and the Laird. Although found guilty, the laird evidently found sympathy in the jury for he was sentenced to pay £10 to the deceased's nearest relatives, provide masses for his victim's eternal soul, and to make a holy pilgrimage to do penance at the shrine of St. John in Amiens, France. Hardly the sternest of sentences, all of which he fulfilled, it is clear that some mitigation was found to have existed, as a punishment of such levity was hardly par for the course in those days, even for the landed gentry!

However, had this been his only "claim to fame" doubtless our man would have been consigned to oblivion, or at best referred to in some obscure legal publication. This was not to be.

His trip to France had an interesting side effect. Having developed his keen business-eye by that time, and after contact with external influences, he returned home in 1534 to set his home town on its path for the future. In 1542 he sought and obtained from King James V a charter for all the fishing rights from Cairnbulg to Coburty. This was the start of our fortunes!

On the 2nd of November, 1546, Alexander received a charter from Queen Mary creating Faithlie a free Burgh of Barony and he began to build a harbour. This was not the spacious bustling port of today, but a formal harbour none the less, and the direct ancestor of the port without which the town of Fraserburgh could not have developed.

As his son Alexander pre-deceased him, passing away in 1564, his grandson, also Alexander, inherited considerable estates, property, wealth and title on his grandfather's death on 12th April, 1569.

This Alexander, the Eighth Laird, history remembers as the founder of our town.

ALEXANDER FRASER, 8th Laird of Philorth

Born around the year 1537, and receiving his education in his early years locally (in the custom of his time for gentry his later education was given to him in Edinburgh) little is known of him until inheriting the title from his grandfather, other than marrying Magdalene Ogilvy in 1559.

On the 6th of March, 1570, he laid the foundation stone of his castle on Kinnaird Head, a place thought worthy of mention by Ptolemy as the Promentorium Taixalium, and in 1571 commenced building a church handily placed to his new home.

After catering for his own spiritual and secular needs, he launched on the building of a new town on the site of the burgh of Faithlie, recently created by his grandfather. His plans for his town were futuristic to say the least envisaging the needs perhaps of present day "flagpolers" by incorporating in his design streets some 40 feet in width. It could be that March held some significance for the farsighted Alex for it was on the 9th of that month in 1576 that he laid the foundation stone to the new part of the harbour — the original part being started by his grandfather.

On the 1st of July 1592 he obtained from his good friend King James the Sixth, or First as he was to be called after the Union of the Crowns, a further charter declaring his new demesne to be a "burgh of regality" ordaining that the town shall be called "in all time coming the burgh and port de Fraser". Thus Fraserburgh was founded.

In 1594 he received from the King a knighthood, to mark the occasion of the baptism of Prince Henry, the King's son.

Such was the pace of development of the new town that its neighbour, Aberdeen, on more than one occasion raised its voice in anger or complaint at the success enjoyed by the Broch, and not just locally, for it complained loud and long to the Government and the Regent about this upstart town in the north.

As history bears witness, the pleas fell on deaf ears as both towns continue to exist side by side — and in greater harmony than in years gone by! No record can be found marking the death of Magdalene, his first wife, but she is not heard of after 1606. Sir Alexander Fraser of Fraserburgh, as he was now known, married Dame Elizabeth Maxwell, Lady Lochinver, the daughter of Queen Mary's friend Sir John Maxwell, in June, 1606.

One cannot forget Sir Alexander's attempt to establish a University in the town in a list of his numerous achievements, not to mention ambitions, for his area. In 1592, building started on an area of ground on the north side of College Bounds and in 1597 an Act of Parliament recognised this achievement and granted its blessing on his venture, along with a grant from the Scotch Parliament of the year. The history of our University is well documented and need not be mentioned further.

Having devoted all his life, which ended in July, 1623, to the creation of his masterpiece, the Broch, he died in relative poverty having expended his vast wealth for the common good.

Suffice to say that without this man, you would not be reading this book and no better epitaph can be given to him than,

> "The King, O Fraserburgh! has given to thee
> A name, through ages known to knightly fame.
> Long flourishing thou! upheld by piety;
> And aye be mindful of thine honoured name."

BILL GIBB

In the sixties and seventies the international world of high fashion was taken by storm by the unique designs of a young Fraserburgh man.

Brought up on Lochpots Farm, Bill was to become one of the world's top fashion designers, producing clothes for the rich and famous, including film and pop stars. He began "designing" when still a twelve year old pupil at Fraserburgh. Encouraged by his family and his art teacher at the Academy, Bill went to St. Martin's School of Art in London where he graduated with honours and was top student of his year.

He gained a scholarship to enter the Royal College of Art and while there, at the age of 23, he opened his first business venture in the form of a small boutique in Kensington. His first fashion show was staged a year later in 1967 and by 1970 he was the winner of the Vogue Designer of the Year Award.

A number of different sources were to hail Bill Gibb as one of the best dress designers of his generation. He was to go on to receive repeated international acclaim for his work but unfortunately, in business terms, he was less than successful.

His company experienced financial problems and in 1978 it collapsed. Undaunted, Bill fought back only to have his business fail once more in 1980. But, despite these setbacks, he went on to create new designs and small collections for some of London's top stores.

A highly talented and creative young man, Bill Gibb developed cancer and died in a London hospital in January, 1988, at the age of 44. Throughout his life he kept in touch with his family and friends in the North-east, frequently visiting the area, and was buried at New Pitsligo where his parents lived.

THOMAS BLAKE GLOVER

Thomas Blake Glover was born in Commerce Street in Fraserburgh on the 6th of June, 1838, and was baptised on the 12th of July in the old St. Peter's Episcopal Church (now the St. Andrew's Hall), in Mid Street.

His father, Thomas Berry Glover, was the Chief Coastguard in Fraserburgh and while stationed at Sandend, Glover senior had met and married Banffshire lass Mary Findlay of Fordyce.

By 1851, the Glovers had moved to the Bridge of Don and, after leaving school in 1854, young Thomas found employment as a Clerk.

Seeking fame and fortune he left Scotland for the Far East, working first in Shanghai for a couple of years and then moving to Japan, arriving in Nagasaki on the 18th of September, 1859.

At this time Japan was in the middle of political turmoil and upheaval which would ultimately see the country pushed into the modern world a decade later — helped considerably by Brocher Thomas Blake Glover.

In 1853 the military dictator, the Shogun had been forced by the great naval powers to end Japan's 250 year-old self-imposed isolation from the rest of the world.

Thomas Blake Glover established himself as an import/export merchant, dealing in tea and other commodities and became very successful in a short space of time.

But these were dangerous times in Japan. For a while in 1862 anti-foreigner feelings ran so high that, after a spate of horrific attacks on Europeans and pro-Western Japanese, traders were forced to live and conduct their business in boats in Nagasaki harbour.

No-one could have blamed Glover if, having made his fortune, he had chosen to leave Japan and the troubles behind him, like so many other get-rich-quick merchants of the day. But, and this is why he is so revered today, he decided to stay. It is no exaggeration to say that by staying he was putting his life in daily danger, but Glover could sense the wind of change blowing through Japan and was instrumental in bringing about that change.

Glover prospered during the civil war, supplying both sides with ships and weapons. His sympathies, however, were with the rebel clans and, looking to the future, he could see the day when Japan would take its place alongside the leading nations of the world. He financed and arranged for the sons of young samurai to to be sent abroad to be educated in the ways of the West. Although foreigners at this time were not subject to Japanese law, Glover, by this beneficent although reactionary act, could have faced persecution, and even death, at the hands of Japanese Kamikaze extremists.

During the mid 1860's, Glover had become the biggest ship owner in Japan. Through links with his ship-broker brothers in Aberdeen he ordered the first three warships for the Japanese Navy which were built by Alexander Hall and Co.

He was responsible for a number of technological innovations in Japan. He introduced the first railway, the first mint, and started the first industrialised mines. Probably his most significant contribution to the modernising of Japan was his establishing of a patent slip dock at Kosuge in Japan. He had it built in Aberdeen, taken apart, then shipped over to Japan in specially designed ships and re-assembled at Kosuge, from where the world's biggest shipping concern, Mitsubishi, was to grow.

The civil war ended in 1868 with the Shogun deposed and the Emperor Meiji restored with his full monarchical powers. Ironically however, Glover suffered because of this. Orders for ships and arms had dried up, loans he had made to others were not repaid, markets were fluctuating and, Glover having overstretched himself financially, his company went bankrupt.

Glover had met Yataro Iwasaki, the founder of Mitsubishi, during the rebellion in April, 1867 when Yataro had come to Nagasaki on an arms-buying mission for his Tosa clan. They became firm friends and one historian described them "as if they were real brothers". The fledgling Mitsubishi company took over Glover's shipping and mining interests and Glover became a highly paid consultant with that firm, advising Mitsubishi during its years of great expansion, reportedly receiving a salary 20% higher than that of the Mitsubishi chairman.

In his spare time Glover was allowed to develop his commercial interests, founding in 1885 the company which makes Kirin Beer, by far the most popular brew in Japan today, accounting for over 50% of the massive Japanese beer market.

Glover became an honoured guest and consultant to the Japanese government in later years and held substantial influence. Many of those in power, and they included a prime minister, several cabinet ministers, as well as leading industrialists and academics, had been the young sons of samurai sent abroad by Glover many years earlier.

In 1908, on the recommendation of Ito Hirobumi, Japan's first prime minister and by now elder statesman, Emperor Meiji awarded Thomas Blake Glover the Order of the Rising Sun, Japan's highest honour and never before given to a non-Japanese. At the presentation ceremony, the official list of Glover's achievements ran to 20 pages of script.

Glover's personal life was colourful to say the least. His second marriage to a poor samurai's daughter, Tsuru Otsuki, lasted more than 30 years, but an affair with another Japanese woman, Maka Kagi, resulted in the birth of a son, Tomisaburo, or Thomas Junior, and gave rise to the "Madam Butterfly" legend.

It is thought that Glover was the role model for Lt. Pinkerton, the American naval officer in Puccini's opera "Madam Butterfly", whose Japanese wife commited suicide in front of their son when deserted by her husband. Tomisaburo was taken into the Glover household when he was six and educated at a methodist mission. The headmaster's wife's brother was John Luther Long who wrote the original play on which Madam Butterfly was based. Years later Long told a soprano that the boy's real name was Tom Glover whose father was an "English Merchant". His mother had attempted suicide but, unlike in the opera, had failed.

Glover died in Tokyo at the age of 73 on the 16th of December, 1911 of Bright's Disease, a kidney ailment, and is buried in Nagasaki. The beautiful house he had built there in 1863 has been preserved as a site of national, historic and cultural importance. Now known as Glover Mansion it is recognised as the first example of western architecture meeting Eastern, and is venerated as a shrine by many Japanese. It stands alongside several other buildings which formed part of the thriving European settlement during the 1860's and is part of the huge Glover Garden tourist complex which attracts more than 2,000,000 visitors annually, paying tribute to the founder of Modern Japan, the young Brocher who lived in Commerce Street.

COLONEL ROBERT (BOB) LOW

To this man, born in the Broch in 1874, indisputably goes the title "the fastest builder in the west", for in a period of only 10 days he built a city from scratch for 30,000 souls.

Born to a plasterer George Low, and a cousin of Mr. W. Cameron, a grocer then operating from Cross Street, Bob as he was known, emigrated to Canada in 1886 aged 12. From 1889 to 1894 we would find him working with his father on various projects among which was the construction of new fortifications near Halifax, Nova Scotia.

However in 1899 greater things were on the horizon for the adventurous Bob. He was asked to construct the mighty Dominion Iron & Steel Company's plant in Sydney, Nova Scotia. This project had our hero managing an incredible 2,500 men and needless to say the intrepid Bob completed the job on time.

In 1911 he was given the task of constructing the Connaught Rifle Range, three times larger than the next largest in the world. While engaged on that task war was declared, and due to these circumstances the Minister of Militia elected to complete this project under his aegis and consigned Colonel Bob to his most exacting task. Within 24 hours of being asked, he removed himself from Ottowa to Valcartier, then a flag stop on the Canadian Northern Railway, with his crack gang of 400 men to construct a city with all amenities capable of housing 30,000 soldiers in only 10 days.

A workaholic and hard taskmaster, he believed it to be essential that his men were well catered for and so the first building to be erected was the kitchen cum dining room, where menus of banquet proportions were available day and night for his workforce. In return for this his men were expected to work from dawn to dusk, but unusually for the time were paid hourly and paid well! Again Bob proved more than equal to the task as the job, incredibly, was completed on time.

After this our builder then completed camps at Sewell in Manitoba, Sarcee in Calgary and Borden, Nova Scotia. His career went full circle when he was asked by the Government to upgrade the fort at Halifax, Nova Scotia, built by his father is 1886!

As is commonly the case with men of this mark, sentiment rarely rears its "ugly head". However, and notwithstanding the wholesale displacement of farmers, Colonel Bob altered the design of the entire camp at Valcartier to allow an elderly woman to remain in her home of many years.

ROBERTSON MACAULAY

Born in 1833 at 50 Shore Street, the son of a Lewis man and Broch quine called Margaret Noble, he first moved home aged 10 to live with his father's sister in Stornoway.

This relative isolation did not suit the young Macaulay who became indentured to a solicitor, one Donald Munro, finishing his legal training in Aberdeen.

Now imbued with the desire to make his fame and fortune, he left Scotland in 1853 for Canada, being followed the next year by his mother, brothers and sisters. Arriving in Hamilton, Ontario, he first was employed by the Canada Life Company where he worked for some time before moving to the employ of the Mutual Life of Canada Assurance Company. After carving a name for himself with that company it became apparent that he was a major talent in his field. Several companies tried to "head-hunt" our man and after much consideration he chose the Sun Life of Canada to which he was appointed Company Secretary in 1874. Upon his entry to their head office, the staff numbered but two people. Now its staff are in uncounted hundreds! When Robertson arrived in 1874 the annual income was £12,059 and the assets were £25,992. By 1911 he had raised these figures to £2,363,354 and £8,777,758, with life assurance in force to the value of £33,816,180, thus making the Sun Life the largest company of its kind anywhere in the Empire.

He died in 1915 having passed custody of the managing director's chair to his son Doctor Thomas B. Macaulay who continued the dynasty for a number of years.

He is remembered to this day by his son's donation to this town of sufficient monies to provide the Macaulay Hall for further generations.

CHARLES RAWDEN MacLEAN

Perhaps no one in this book better personifies the traditional Broch traits of indominatibility and the ability to triumph over adversity than this bold lad. Born in Fraserburgh on 17th August, 1815, virtually two months to the day after the Battle of Waterloo, he was almost thrust on to the pathway to greatness by circumstances totally outwith his control, not that it seems he would have wished for a different fate.

MacLean is recorded in the diary of Henry Francis Fynn who, as the partner of Lt. Francis Farewell, achieved fame through his dealings with Shaka, as being the apprentice of James Saunders King, another of Farewell's partners, on King's ship the brig "Mary". The "Mary" was shipwrecked in 1825 at Natal but, notwithstanding this unfortunate act of God, King and his entourage set about the establishment of a British outpost at Port Natal with mixed degrees of success.

By this time MacLean had changed his name, as people of that time were wont to do, often for reasons best left forgotten, to John Ross. Mention the name MacLean in South Africa and you may be greeted by a blank stare, but mention the name John Ross and it will be instantly associated with this heroic Brocher. McLean and others of his party, by dint of the fact that they had appropriated a piece of Zulu empire to build this outpost, had formed an association with, and indeed some had been befriended by, King Shaka. Shaka was the man who singlehandedly had amalgamated a handful of rival and warring tribes into the Zulu Nation, and in so doing had provided the world with arguably the finest light infantry in history, and the British Empire with one of her most implacable foes.

Ross, as he was known by this time, had it appears assumed this name because of his long red hair. This impressed Shaka greatly, the king proclaiming it to be like the tail of a steer. Hardly flattering, but as we are told that this was the only red hair in South Africa, it doubtless seemed a natural parallel for Shaka to make.

Shaka was fairly taken with Ross, and we know of his entrancement with Ross's ability to dance a 'Scottish hornpipe' while dressed in his sailor suit.

His employer James King, a thoroughly unscrupulous man with an eye for the main chance, sold John Ross to Shaka as a personal body servant in exchange for Durban Bluff, a piece of land destined through course of time to become one of the most valuable pieces of property in the world. Ritter records that Shaka really loved the boy and adopted him as his own son, treating him well and with honour for the duration of their association. A touching example of his protectiveness is shown by his command that the boy be plastered from head to foot with mud at all times, as his fair skin burnt easily causing terrible suffering to the young lad.

Ross is distinguished among his contemporaries by being the only one to become fluent in the difficult Zulu language, and so accustomed in its use did he become, that we are told when he returned to the Bay (Natal) he had almost forgotten how to speak English, and had totally forgotten his father's native Gaelic. This suggests that his parents hailed from the west coast or the islands, but there is no doubt that our man was a Brocher as he is recorded for all to see as being born in the town, in the Parish Register of Births, Deaths and Marriages.

He became, through his close association with Shaka, the only white to regularly witness Zulu affairs and was often present at the formation of the Zulu imperium. His fluency in Zulu qualified him well as official translator and mediator between King Shaka and the British, a duty he was often asked to perform, which no doubt gave him an unequalled insight to the working of Shaka and his court.

By 1827 it is reported that the situation at the Port had deteriorated to such an extent that survival of the colony depended on the acquisition of various "essentials". It must be remembered that this was an outpost on the edge of white civilisation and succour was not available round the corner. After petitioning Shaka for assistance, which the King was pleased to give, much discussion took place among the European Community as to who would "go to the shops".

Ross did not hesitate! Aged 12 years old, and having already experienced more adventure than most men could do in a few lifetimes, he volunteered to make the trip to the Portuguese settlement at Delagoa Bay, a round trip of 600 miles through some of the most hostile country in the world, and at that time untravelled by any European. Nathaniel Issacs, one of the colonists, records that "Ross, a shrewd and active lad of about 15 years old was appointed to make the trek", justifying the trip by stating that "a mere boy travelling alone would not excite the King's (Shaka) suspicions". Although this stands as a tribute in itself, as the Europeans would have sent the lad on his journey alone, it does not recognise the friendship that existed between Ross and Shaka. Shaka, obviously aware of the dangers that his adopted son would face, provided both troops to escort and protect him and food to sustain him on his travels, as well as arranging safe passage through country controlled by rival tribes.

Far from being the personification of evil as Shaka was portrayed at the time, and unfortunately it is this "memory" that survives all others, the King at that time went out of his way to appease the colonists in an attempt to establish a cordial relationship with, and be seen as an equal by, King George IV. It was Shaka's greatdesire that the two kings should live in peace and harmony. Georgie, as he was called by Shaka, did not have either Shaka's foresight or "civilisation" and history bears witness to numerous attempts by the British to humiliate, subjugate, and conquer the Zulu nation.

On Ross's arival at Delagoa Bay he was well and kindly received by the Portuguese but nonetheless they thought that he must be a spy for the Zulus, as "surely no Christian would countenance sending a mere boy on such a trip".

John proved to be something of an accomplished trader for he managed to purchase all the goods required back in Port Natal for the expenditure of a mere 2 dollars! The volume of goods purchased were of such quantity that 10 hardy Zulus were required to carry them back. A canny mannie this laddie! There is more than the merest suspicion that young John made all his purchases from the captain of a French slaver, the notorious Dorval of Mauritius. There is great irony in the fact that the boy should deal with such a man, even to save his fellow colonists, for at 16 he was sailing a brig of his own with a multi-racial crew of freed slaves in a personal war against all slave traders.

When Jackabo, as the Zulus called John, returned, they bestowed on him the title I-Qawu which translates to the Hero, a most apt epithet indeed.

In 1828 Shaka was murdered and the Zulu nation collapsed, albeit temporarily, into disarray bordering on chaos, with the whites waiting in the wings to take capital advantage from any opportunity. John devoted the rest of his life to the cause of black liberty and equality and was determined in his fight against slavery in all its forms. He particularly singled out his old friend Issacs, who by this time had fulfilled his destiny by becoming a slaver of some notoriety, being responsible for the fates of tens of thousands of unfortunate black souls.

At this time one of the major slave markets was found in America so without further ado John sailed off to the Caribbean, with his motley crew attacking and destroying all black ships that crossed his path in order to rescue their human cargo.

One of the incidents he was involved in while persecuting this odious trade contributed directly to the outbreak of the largest modern war against slavery, the American Civil War.

MacLean never returned to Africa, making his home in St. Lucia where he remained for the rest of his life.

Obtaining his master's ticket in 1833 he initially was employed by a planter called Henry King commanding the barque "Sandwich". When King had a new vessel built in 1838, "a fine, new, coppered and copper fastened brig" called "Susan", after King's wife, he placed his most trusted man in command, Charles MacLean. Onward and upward went MacLean's maritime career for in 1844 he took command of the barque "Gilbert Munro" for King. Described as a fine ship of 258 tons MacLean ran sugar for his employer on the London-St. Lucia route. When the Mercantile Marine Act called for a formal ticketing system to be introduced for sailors on 26th August, 1852, Certificate of Competence (No. 6835), class, Ordinary Master, bore the name Charles Rawden MacLean, "competent to command any vessel of whatsoever tonnage".

The precise date of MacLean's marriage is not known but it is a matter of record that in 1856 his wife accompanied him on the "Gilbert Munro" to the Crimea with a load of building materials consigned to the front at Balaclava — King's finest vessel had been commandeered as a transport ship. By the early 1860s MacLean captained a cutter called "Liver" founding the St. Lucia Steamship Conveyance Company (Ltd.), running sugar in a small fleet of two ships, the "Aid" and the "Creole" to London. MacLean was also a writer of some note, among his works being the first definitive work on his home in St. Lucia, covering aspects as varied as its history, geography, current status and future prospects. It is documented in the "St. Lucia Observer" that by 1874 he was the coroner for the island's First District, stipendiary magistrate for the island and chairman of the Poor House Committee which administered both the General and Mental Hospitals, holding these positions until he fell ill on 20th March, 1880. He was never to recover from this illness, and although his death is unrecorded we know that he left this mortal coil between January, 1882 and March, 1886.

If memorials testify to greatness, then the number and diversity of those dedicated to this Broch man place him among Kings and Emperors. Not only has he made his mark on the world as a humanitarian, mariner, legislator, historian, author and man of principle, he has been honoured in his John Ross personna in his beloved Africa. Among these "memorials" are the John Ross pool on the Durban esplanade, opened in 1956; 1958 saw part of the Eshowe highway named in his honour; 1959 had the bridge over the Tugela River dedicated in his name. The old fort at Durban carries a plaque honouring the young lad of the trek and the "John Ross" tug skittles bravely round Durban Harbour. There is an immense block of flats called John Ross House with a magnificent mural depicting the youthful John with his Zulu friends, fronted by a superb bronze statue. Richards' Bay has remembered him by naming a school the John Ross College. In literature, as well as being remembered for his own works, he is immortalised in Gutteridge's book "Thunder over Africa"; in "Natalia" he figures prominently among the early and important pioneers; and Schroeder honours him by casting him with a pantheon of great Afrikaaner heroes in his "Bravery in South Africa — Stories from our Heroic Past". MacLean is also the first Brocher to be honoured by both television and the silver screen. SABC-TV have a popular children's serial — "John Ross: An African Adventure", and there is currently a film being made, again in South Africa, on his colourful and eventful life. While this list of honours is long and varied it is by no means exhaustive but to collate all of them would take more space than this small volume allows.

When John Dalrymple and his wife Isabell bore witness to his baptism in 1815 by the Reverend Gardiner, they could not have suspected that Charles Rawden MacLean, the son of a Royal Navy Lieutentant, would make such a mark on the world.

JOHN C. MILNE

Yet another famous Brocher, and what a man this is! A country loon, born in Memsie and learning his three R's at the local school, he had a passionate interest in people and the countryside round about him.

Most of us recognise the farm names he uses so readily because they were close to him both geographically and affectionately — Pickerstane, Newseat, Bodychell, Whitewell, Kirkton and Mains of Pittendrum (or "Pittendree").

He could describe so succinctly the very character of Buchan as seen through the eyes of the farm worker — "The Orra Loon".

> *"Fin I'm rowein oot the muck and tummle owre a sharny neep*
> *And lat the coupit barra skliter ben the skliddery greep*
> *I winna say that Sklarverdads flang oot her orra leg*
> *And gart that barra skite like fut Meggie daes a 'gleg,*
> *For that wad be as muckle as te say it wasna me,*
> *Fin I am aince the orra loon at Mains o' Pittendree."*

Reminiscing about Primary schooldays —

> *"It's jist a fortnicht noo or I maun leave the Memsie Skweel*
> *Gweed fa' the sonsie wifie that has tried to learn me weel!*
> *I'll mebbe think upon her wi' a tear-drap in my ee*
> *Fin I am aince the orra loon at Mains o' Pittendree."*

John C. Milne continued his education at Fraserburgh Academy and went on to Aberdeen University where he distinguished himself by graduating First Class Honours in Mental Philosophy, following this with First Class Honours in Moral Philosophy while lecturing in Logic at King's College in Aberdeen.

About ten years later he became interested in geography and again obtained First Class Honours, which gained him the post of Principal Lecturer in Geography at Aberdeen University.

In 1939, whilst still Principal Lecturer he became Headmaster of the Demonstration School, Aberdeen, and in 1952 was made Principal Master of Method at Aberdeen College of Education.

Sadly, just before he was due to retire at sixty-five, he died on December 3rd, 1962.

He had amassed such a wealth of poems apart from "The Orra Loon", which was the only one published within his lifetime, that a colleague, Miss Nan Shepherd, took in hand to edit them with the help of his wife and daughter, for publication in December, 1963. Within four days the thousand copies were sold out! This was a phenomenal success for a book which appeared to have such a limited potential appeal. Needless to say it was reprinted in paperback in 1976 and again in 1978.

Despite that popularity, today we can almost hear the great man say : —
> *"Faurs the bonnie dialect*
> *That aince wis spoken here?"*

KENNETH MINTY

The Broch has produced not only a Treasurer of the Bank of Scotland in Sir George Anderson but also a chief accountant of that Institute in Mr Kenneth Minty.

During the first world war, when it was difficult to recruit apprentices, an eagle-eyed agent of the Bank of Scotland saw a promising trainee in Kenneth Minty. Thus he was encouraged to leave school at fourteen and embark on a career with the local bank.

He soon justified the agent's confidence for within four years he had passed both the Associates' and the Members' examinations and was appointed accountant at the local branch the following year. In 1922 aged 18, he moved from the Broch to become accountant at Macduff. Two years later he was transferred to Glasgow, spending eight months at Maryhill before becoming accountant in the newly opened branch at Blytheswoood.

His promotion to an Inspector of Branches in 1928 at the age of 25 was indicative of his ability and talent. By 1946 he had moved to the Chief Accountant's Department as assistant Chief Accountant. Eight years later when the Bank of Scotland and the Union Bank were preparing to merge, Mr. Minty was appointed Chief Accountant of the Union Bank and when the amalgamation of the two institutes was completed in 1955 he was to become Chief Accountant of the combined bank.

Despite the many complex changes which were to take place in the banking world in the subsequent years Mr. Minty was equal to the challenge — a master of his craft.

When time permitted he would relax on the golf course. In his younger days he had been a keen footballer but golf remained his favourite pastime. The first bonus he ever received from the bank, the princely sum of £5, enabled him to buy a full set of golf clubs. With a handicap of three he obviously applied the same concentration and dedication to his hobby as he did to his work.

Returning to Fraserburgh in 1967, he remained living out his retirement at 28 Victoria Street until his death on 20th May, 1978.

MAGNUS MOWATT

Born in the Broch in May, 1841, he became a member of the Legislative Council of India in 1879 and is noted by Cranna as "a man among ten thousand".

Mowatt left school in the town aged 15, and studied law in Edinburgh till aged 21. He was then sent to India in 1866 by his employers, Findlay Campbell & Company, where he became, as well as a leading light in the business community, a Justice of the Peace and chairman of the Bombay Chamber of Commerce.

In 1875 he propounded the then novel theory that gold be used as a basis for currency, which not unsurprisingly won notice and acclaim in the press and financial institutions.

After returning to these shores in 1880, he became a director in numerous esteemed companies and became acknowledged as a poet of "remarkable" ability.

PETER NOBLE

Perhaps Fraserburgh's foremost linguist, he was born in 1899 the son of Mr. Andrew Noble, a cooper. After getting a thorough Broch Academy education (a standard still maintained today), he went as the Academy's first bursar to Aberdeen University, graduating in 1916 having won every Latin and Greek prize available. Moving then to Cambridge he was credited with First Class Honours in both Classical and Oriental languages.

After lecturing at Liverpool and Leeds Universities, he returned to chair the Humanities Faculties in Aberdeen. He was twice awarded the Bendall Sanskritt Scholarship, and was a co-editor of a major academic work translating the Kharosthi Inscriptions. He was later appointed, in 1952, Principal of King's College at the University of London and held this post along with that of Vice Chancellor until his retirement in 1958. Knighted in 1967, he will be best remembered by his students for his humanity and a genuine interest in the man.

JIM PARK

Jim Park? Aye at's richt, Jim Park!

This Jim Park was a brother of our ex-provost John Park and was a well-known shipowner of his time. He was born in 1828 and graduated M.A. from Aberdeen University. After graduation he moved to London to run the extensive shipping business owned by his father, eventually being elected to Lloyd's committee.

In 1873 he chaired the General Shipowner's Society, a position he must have held successfully, being re-elected in the same capacity in 1880. He was also a director of the then notable shipping company of Shaw, Saville and Albion until his death aged 65 in 1893.

His dying wish was that his ashes be placed in a bottle, which was to be handed to the master of the first ship of his line leaving London. The master was then to point his bows to face the Broch, break the bottle and scatter his remains to the four winds. Not surprisingly, this request was carried out in honour of this most respected of men.

JAMES RAMSAY

One of the first people in Britain to speak out publicly against the slave trade, James Ramsay was a pioneer in the early history of the abolition movement. He was a major influence on Wilberforce, Clark and Pitt, the famous figures usually associated with the abolition of slavery.

Born in Fraserburgh on 25th July, 1733, Ramsay received his early education locally before entering King's College, Aberdeen, to study medicine. On graduating he then spent two years in London studying pharmacy and surgery. On completion of the course he joined the Royal Navy as a surgeon.

Ramsay's first contact with the slave trade came in 1759. While Acting Surgeon on the "Arundel" commanded by Sir Charles Middleton, the fleet was requested to assist a slaver infested with plague. No surgeon was willing to expose himself to the contagion other than Ramsay. Without regard to personal safety, he boarded the ship, treated the patients as best he could and, on leaving, left written instructions for their future treatment. The conditions he encountered on the slave ship left a lasting impression on him.

Unfortunately, on returning to his own ship, he fell on deck and broke his thigh bone. This left him lame and forced him to resign from the Navy.

Ramsay's first calling had been the Church and, on hearing of a vacancy at St. Kitts, he returned to London to be ordained. A recommendation by his former commander and friend, Sir Charles Middleton, ensured Ramsay's entry to the

Church and in 1762 he took charge of the parishes of Christchurch, Nicolatown, and St. John's Capisterre in St. Kitts.

In 1763 he married Miss Rebecca Akers, a Creole and daughter of a wealthy planter. They had four children — three girls and a boy, the son pre-deceasing Ramsay.

For the next nineteen years Ramsay worked hard as both doctor and minister to alleviate the suffering of the slaves. In doing so he incurred the wrath and bitter hatred of the plantation owners who were to persecute him for the rest of his life.

By 1777 things became so bad that Ramsay returned to Britain on a visit, hoping his absence might defuse the intolerable situation. He spent three weeks in Scotland, including a visit to Fraserburgh to see his sister and family.

The following year he served as Chaplain, for a short spell, with the Royal Navy in the West Indies. On resigning his commission he returned to St. Kitts. Finding the opposition stronger than ever he finally retired to England in 1781 with his wife, family and personal servant, Nestor.

He immediately took up the livings of Teston and Nettlestead offered to him by Sir Charles Middleton who lived nearby at Barham Court. The Middletons had many influential visitors at Barham Court including William Pitt and William Wilberforce, then a young M.P.

Over the next few years, many meetings and discussions on the subject of slavery took place at Teston. Lady Middleton encouraged Ramsay to revise and expand a memorial of his personal experiences of the slave trade in the West Indies, which he published in 1784. The publication, "An Essay on the Treatment and Conversion of African Slaves in the British Sugar Colonies", was a damning indictment of the British West Indian slave trade. It attracted much public attention and support for the early abolitionists.

But the essay also fired the hostility of the West Indian planters and during the next few years Ramsay had to defend himself against many vindictive attacks. The onslaught on Ramsay's character was spearheaded by James Tobin and resulted in a long-running pamphlet war from which Ramsay finally emerged the victor. The controversy attracted considerable interest and one positive outcome was that the general public became more aware of the inhumanity and impolicy of the West Indian slave trade.

Meanwhile the abolitionist cause was gaining strength. The Quakers had petitioned the House of Commons; Sir Charles Middleton had approached the young Wilberforce to champion the cause in Parliament; and Thomas Clarkson was introduced to Ramsay and, having spent a month with him at Teston, resolved to devote himself to the cause. A national movement was formed in 1787 headed by Granville Sharp — their sole purpose, to promote the cause throughout the country and plan a parliamentary campaign.

William Pitt and William Wilberforce, relying heavily on Ramsay to advise them, raised the matter in the House of Commons in 1788. Several debates took place but it was 12th May, 1789, before the motion was finally raised in full debate. During the debate a Mr. Molyneaux, an M.P., and owner of a West Indian sugar plantation, made a vicious attack on Ramsay's character.

Ramsay had been ill for a short time but had never eased up on his life-long fight against slavery. He ably defended himself and his cause, knowing that his time was limited and yet fully satisfied that his life's work had not been in vain.

Ramsay died on 20th July, 1789, at the London home of Sir Charles Middleton and was buried five days later at Teston. His battle was over, but the war on slavery had just begun. As an early pioneer, who alone knew from personal experience what slavery meant in human terms, James Ramsay should be remembered and honoured for the considerable contribution he made to the abolition of slavery.

16th LORD SALTOUN

Alexander George Fraser, perhaps the Broch's most famous "sodger", upheld the valiant traditions of his ancestors, such as Simon Fraser who fought with William Wallace in 1302, Sir Alexander Fraser who played his part at Bannockburn and lost his life at Duplin in 1332, another Sir Alexander who fell with King James III at Sauchieburn and yet another Sir Alexander who aided King Charles II at Worcester.

The 16th Lord joined up in 1802 aged 17, fought his way through Sicily, Corunna, the Peninsular campaign of Wellington, Nivelle, Nive, Bayonne, Quatre Bras, Peronne, and had his greatest hour assisting Sir John MacDonnel in the defence of Hougomont at Waterloo. As any scholar of this period will testify, the retention of this key position was critical to the success of the British and Allied army that fateful day.

Although the 16th Lord did not play second fiddle to anyone on the battlefield, he was an extremely accomplished violinist as well as being an acclaimed and adept parliamentarian.

He was nicely summed up by no less a person than the Iron Duke, Wellington himself, as being a pattern to the army "both as a man and a soldier".

STEWART SLESSOR

Born on the 2nd of November 1912, the son of Dr. Robert Slessor the local physician, and educated at Fraserburgh Academy, Aberdeen Grammar School then graduating M.B. Ch.B. at Aberdeen University, Stewart Slessor gained his greatest fame in climates even colder than he had experienced in the Broch.

Initially specialising in gynaecology, he was assistant master in one of the world's leading gynaecological hospitals, the Rotunda in Dublin. He joined the service of the R.N.V.R. in the early days of the last war with the rank of Surgeon Lieutenant Commander, and saw active service on a destroyer "H.M.S. Wanderer", gaining a mention in dispatches for his skilful amputation of a seaman's leg during a storm.

On his appointment to RN Sick Quarters in 1943 he was to meet the man who opened his door to Antartica, his chief, Surgeon Commander E.W. "Ted" Bingham. Bingham had seen service in Antartica before the outbreak of war and was a natural choice to lead an expedition at the invitation of the Colonial office.

In the spring of 1945, and with a team of his choosing, Stewart Slessor being appointed second-in-command and base doctor, Bingham set off. His mission was to study the continent's geography and climate, and to explore the 5,000 foot high plateau on the peninsula. Bingham was injured and returned to base camp in Marguerite Bay, leaving Slessor in command of a three-man party who were commissioned to traverse the peninsula by dog-sled, to further their studies. They returned to Marguerite Bay in 1947 having been where no man had ever set foot before. For this intrepid journey he was awarded the rare Polar Medal, the only medal with a snow white ribbon.

After a short sojourn in England he sailed on the "John Briscoe" as advisor to the redoubtable Vivian Fuchs, returning after the first part of the voyage, having fulfilled his duties. In 1948 Slessor was appointed as a senior medical officer to the Colonial Service in the Falkland Islands, a position he held until his retirement 20 years later. During this time he was awarded the OBE for service in the Falklands and had a mountain in Antartica, Mount Slessor, named in his honour.

His untimely death in the Cairngorms, while hillwalking on 8th July 1985 near Mar Lodge, robbed the nation of an explorer who was able to be ranked alongside Scott & Shackleton. His remains were, according to his wishes, interred alongside his wife's in Port Stanley cemetery where the spot is marked by a memorial tablet made in Fraserburgh by a local sculptor.

JAMES WALKER

A nephew of James Ramsay, who is referred to elsewhere in this book, he was born on the 24th of January 1770 and, thanks to a bequest from his famous uncle, he was able to study for the ministry. He was educated at Marischal College in Aberdeen then moved to St. John's College in Cambridge from where he graduated B.A. in 1793, M.A. in 1796 and D.D. in 1826.

Aged 23 he was ordained in the capacity of deacon to the Scottish Episcopal Church, but this was only the start of his religious career. In the late 1790's he travelled to Germany as companion and tutor to Sir John Hope and remained in his employ for two or three years.

On his return from Germany, where he was befriended by some of the most eminent scholars of the time, he was ordained as a priest and was placed in charge of St. Peter's Chapel in Auld Reekie. He was distinguished and will be immortalised by becoming the first Protestant minister to regularly hold services in Rome, the seat and stronghold of Catholicism. Returning to Edinburgh in 1829 he resigned his position at St. Peter's, knowing that great things were in store.

On the 7th of March 1830 he was consecrated both as Bishop of Edinburgh and the first Pantonian professor at the Scottish Episcopalian College. The latter office he held until his death on the 5th March 1841. On the resignation of George Gleig, James was elected primus of the Scottish Episcopal Church, the highest position his church could offer.

Like many men of "pairts" he did not content himself with one occupation. Among his secular achievements, his work in the publication of the Encyclopaedia Britt-annica 3rd Edition as sub-editor to the aforementioned George Gleig, then Bishop of Brechin, must place him among the greatest academics that the Broch has produced.

CHRISTIAN WATT

Christian Watt was born at 72 Broadsea on 26th February 1833, the daughter of James Watt, Fisherman, and Helen Noble. She was the seventh of eight children and the first daughter. The family was very poor, but very proud and hard-working.

Christian Watt's legacy is an extraordinary journal, begun in the Aberdeen Royal Mental Asylum in 1880, recalling her life. This was edited by author and historian Sir David Fraser, a descendant of the Frasers of Philorth, (from whom Christian Watt's family also claim descent) and published in 1983 by Paul Harris Publishing as "The Christian Watt Papers".

The journal paints a vivid picture of the grim realities of life for the fisher folk of the North-East during the last century, when working people slaved simply to scrape a living. For Christian this meant entering domestic service at the age of eight and travelling from village to village throughout the Buchan area to sell fish from the age of nine.

In common with others in her position, the spring and summer of her year would be spent away from home, supporting the menfolk fishing on the West Coast or elsewhere. During the autumn she would travel from place to place, selling fish, going as far afield as Upper Deeside. Once the fish had all been disposed of, the women would find employment on a local farm, helping with the hairst. Domestic service with the local gentry, helping out during the shooting season, taking in laundry or gathering shellfish from the shore all helped to supplement a meagre income. This all fitted in with giving birth to and raising large families.

The local aristocrats who lived well on inherited wealth and on levies extracted from the working classes angered Christian Watt, and her outspokenness brought her into open conflict with many of the well-to-do families with which she came into contact.

Despite all she had to endure, Christian did all she could to acquire an education, attending during the slacker winter months the school at Broadsea until she was 20 years old. This learning, allied to the knowledge gleaned from the many people she met and the experiences of her travels, made her very knowledgeable about the history of the area and the local families, the Saltouns and the Frasers, and very aware of different people, lands, languages and customs. Following her father and husband, James, she visited, amongst other places, the West coast of Scotland, the Hebrides and Shetland. Her time in domestic service took her to Edinburgh and London and, in pursuit of an inheritance from her brother, she travelled to New York, where she stayed for 8 months, working in domestic service. This work also included serving at parties for the richest families in the USA.

However, by the age of 47, the constant strain of battling to make a living for herself and her family, and the death of a son and her husband, began to take a toll on her mental health. For the next few years she spent periods of time in Cornhill until, after a final, major breakdown in 1879, she spent the remainder of her life there. Her time was spent working in the laundry and buying fish for the hospital at the fish market in Aberdeen.

During her lifetime, Christian Watt witnessed great changes. The Agricultural and Industrial Revolutions affected greatly the lot of the working people. Many of her family and friends lost relatives during the Crimean War, the Boer War and the Great War, and she describes and comments on all these major world events in her diary.

Against all the odds Christian Watt was an intelligent, well-educated woman with an extraordinarily wide knowledge. She was frank and outspoken, a battler against injustice and a woman of strong religious principles. She died in her 91st year at Aberdeen Royal Mental Asylum, Cornhill. Three of her sons were at her bedside.

WILLIAM WHYTE

Fraserburgh-born pensioners are amongst those who stand to gain most from the generosity of a local baker who made his fortune in South Africa.

William Whyte was the eighth son of Peter Whyte who had a baker's business in Cross Street. He served his apprenticeship with his father and went on to establish a bakery business at the corner of Commerce Street. In 1901, with several of his brothers, he emigrated to South Africa and founded a bakery business in Durban.

The business prospered and, it is understood, by "cornering" the sugar market in South Africa at the start of World War I, the Whyte brothers made a substantial fortune. William retired shortly after the war and gained something of a reputation for his generosity towards War Funds. While on a visit to Fraserburgh he presented the Golf Club with four shelters as well as contributing to the Club's coffers.

On his death in 1942, he left a complex will which provided for various annuities, and on the death of the last annuitant the estate was to be paid over to the former Fraserburgh Town Council. Amongst the provisions for the town was to have been the monies to build a swimming pool and gymnasium, the balance going into a fund called the "Margaret Whyte Fund" after his mother.

Unfortunately, because of the order in which the annuitants had died, the bequest for the swimming pool could not be fulfilled and all the fund became available to the "Margaret Whyte Fund". The last annuitant died in 1984 and three years later the District Council received £128,000 for the Fund. Payments from the Fund are made to persons born in Fraserburgh, and still living in it, who receive a State Pension.

ACKNOWLEDGEMENTS

Among others we gratefully thank the following for their valuable and substantial assistance to the writers in the compilation of this book.

Mrs. J. Arnott

Banff & Buchan District Council

Miss A. Benzie

A. J. & D. R. Cooper, Printers

Dr. E. Gilchrist

Professor S. Gray

Rev. John Green

Margaret Harper

Mr. G. Howatt

Mr. J. Lindsay

Mr. W. Macdonald

Mr. A. McKay

Mrs. S. McRobbie

Miss G. Minty

Mr. J. Marshall

Press & Journal

Mr. W. Watson

Sir James Watt